Superb Steak Recipes

A Complete Cookbook of Delectable Steak Dish Ideas!

Table of Contents

Introduction

What is the best way to prepare your steaks? Should you use a marinade or a dry rub?

Some people who love steaks are adamant in wanting either margination or rubs. But it's more than just a personal preference – some cuts of meat simply cook to a more delicious dinner with one or the other type of preparation.

Marinades and rubs are BOTH good choices for steak. Both of them enhance flavor. Rubs are faster, but sometimes marinades are more effective.

Marinades enhance the flavor of your beef steaks. They are strong, liquid flavor mixtures made with spices and herbs. You'll steep your steaks in them until they take on some of the delicious flavor. You can marinade for just an hour but leaving your steaks to marinate overnight often works best.

Marinades arguably tenderize meats, and some chefs think it does a lot, while others feel that it doesn't do much tenderizing at all. Using a marinade may make a tough cut of meat taste better, but it won't turn the toughest cuts into tender cuts.

Rubs are mixtures of seasoning and spices that are simply rubbed onto a raw meat's surface. Rubs will flavor the meat. Rubs create a savory crust on your steaks, and marinades don't do that. Rubs seal the meat's juiciness in, too.

If you have time before cooking, marinating is great. If you're short on time, try a rub.

Steak isn't just for meals later in the day. There are some great breakfast recipes that feature steak, too. Here are a few...

1 – Chimichurri Breakfast Steak and Eggs

If you think breakfast is an important meal, this is a dish to serve often. It's topped with a tasty herb sauce that really brings out the taste.

Makes 2 Servings

Cooking + Prep Time: 1/2 hour

Ingredients:

For chimichurri

- 1/4 cup of chopped parsley, flat-leaf, fresh
- 1/4 cup of chopped oregano, fresh
- 4 sprigs of mint, fresh
- 2 minced cloves of garlic
- 1/4 cup of oil, olive
- 1/2 lime, juice only
- Salt, kosher
- Pepper, black, fresh ground
- A pinch of pepper flakes, red

For eggs steak

- 1 x 6-oz. sirloin or rib-eye (bone-in) steak
- Salt, kosher
- Pepper, black, fresh ground
- 2 tbsp. of butter, unsalted + more if needed
- 2 eggs, large

Instructions:

1. To prepare chimichurri, combine all those ingredients in medium sized bowl. Incorporate fully by stirring. Set the bowl aside.

2. To prepare eggs steak, season steak as desired. In large sized, heavy skillet, melt butter on med-high. Place steak to one side of skillet and allow space for eggs. Cook till steak is seared dark brown. If pan becomes dry, you can add an extra tbsp. of butter.

3. Reduce heat down to med-low. Add eggs. Season as desired. When whites begin setting, cover skillet and cook for two to three more minutes. Serve meal with chimichurri sauce.

2 – Steak Cheese Breakfast Toast

This toast breakfast is a hearty and rich recipe filled with the best flavors of a brunch. The tender steak is layered on cheesy toast, then topped with an egg.

Makes 4 Servings

Cooking + Prep Time: 25 minutes

Ingredients:

- 4 pcs. of French bread, thick
- 5 ounces of shredded cheddar cheese, sharp
- 6 tbsp. of room temp. butter, unsalted
- 10 ounces of strip steak, New York
- Kosher salt, as desired
- Pepper, ground, as desired
- 3 diced onions, green

Instructions:

1. Season steak as desired.

2. Place 2 tbsp. of butter in large sized skillet on med-high. Cook steak till it is done as you desire.

3. When steak has finished cooking, set on cutting board. Allow to rest for five minutes or a bit longer.

4. Use 2 more tbsp. of butter and butter sides of French bread. Add to separate skillet on med. heat. Cook each side for one to two minutes, till toasted a golden-brown color. Top toast with cheese.

5. In skillet used for steak, lower temp. to low. Add 2 tbsp. butter. Crack eggs gently into pan. Don't allow them to touch.

6. Cook eggs in uncovered pan for five to six minutes, till whites have set. If there is extra butter still in pan, spoon it over eggs while they cook.

7. Slice steak in pieces of 1/4" thickness, against the grain. Layer steak on cheese toast. Top with cooked egg. Season as desired and sprinkle with green onions. Serve promptly.

3 – Egg Steak Breakfast Hash

This could be breakfast – or dinner! The pan-fried potatoes with onions are topped with the eggs, tomatoes and sliced steak for a wonderful meal.

Makes 6 Servings

Cooking + Prep Time: 50 minutes

Ingredients:

- 1 sliced steak, beef sirloin
- 1 lb. of small-cubed potatoes

- Kosher salt, as desired
- Pepper, ground, as desired
- 1 chopped onion, sweet
- 4 large eggs
- 1 cup of halved cherry tomatoes
- Italian seasoning, dry

Instructions:

1. Cook steak in cast iron skillet on med. heat. Flip halfway through till it cooks through evenly. Remove to plate. Reserve drippings in skillet.

2. Add potatoes to same skillet. Season as desired.

3. Stir occasionally while cooking till potatoes are tender. This usually takes between 8 and 12 minutes.

4. Add onion. Cook till browned lightly. By this time potatoes should be fully cooked.

5. Cut the steak in pieces. Return it to skillet and reduce heat down to low.

6. Make four shallow indentations in potato mixture. Crack one egg in each.

7. Scatter tomatoes in skillet. Cover. Cook till egg whites have set but yolks still are runny.

8. Season eggs as desired and sprinkle with the Italian seasoning. Serve.

4 – Egg Steak Breakfast Tacos

This is a Mexican recipe classic that has been cleverly remade to be a great breakfast. It's topped with salsa, guacamole and sour cream – tasty!

Makes 6 Servings

Cooking + Prep Time: 40 minutes

Ingredients:

- 12 oz. of 3/4" thick boneless top sirloin beef steak
- 2 tsp. of oil, vegetable

- 6 x 6" tortillas, flour, warmed
- 6 beaten eggs, large
- 6 tbsp. each of cheddar cheese shreds, reduced-fat; guacamole; salsa and sour cream

Instructions:

1. Heat a large sized, heavy skillet on med. heat. Season the steak as you desire. Place it in the skillet. Pan-broil the steak, turning occasionally, for 12-15 minutes if you prefer your steaks done med-rare or medium. Remove steak from the skillet. Set it aside, keeping it warm.

2. Heat the oil in the same skillet on med. heat. Add the eggs. Scramble till they have set and stir occasionally. Keep them warm, as well.

3. Carve the steak in thin slices and top the tortillas with roughly the same amounts of steak and eggs, and one tbsp. each cheese, salsa, guacamole sour cream. Serve.

5 – Filipino Steak Breakfast

This recipe is deceptively easy, and it's still such a tasty breakfast. Use a tender steak cut that is sliced thinly and chilled with brown sugar and garlic overnight.

Makes 1 Serving

Cooking + Prep Time: 20 minutes + 8 hours chilling time

Ingredients:

- 2 pounds of sirloin steak
- 1 tbsp. of garlic, minced
- 2 tbsp. of sugar, brown
- 1/2 tsp. of pepper, black, ground
- 1 1/2 tbsp. of salt, kosher

Instructions:

1. Mix sugar, kosher salt, ground pepper and garlic together. Spread mixture on steak. Put it in the fridge overnight.

2. The next day, broil or bake your steak and serve.

Steak has always been a favorite main ingredient for some of the tastiest, heartiest lunches, dinners, appetizers and side dishes... Try some soon!

6 – Thai Steak Wraps

This is a wonderful twist on steak salad. The lettuce leaves will wrap up the Thai-infused vegetables and lovingly grilled steak for a great lunch or dinner.

Makes 4 Servings

Cooking + Prep Time: 35 minutes

Ingredients:

- 10 ounces of beans, green
- Flank steak, grilled

- 1 pint of tomatoes, cherry
- 1/2 small onion, red
- 1 cup of mint leaves, fresh
- 1 cup of cilantro, fresh
- 1/2 cup of vinaigrette, soy
- 1 tbsp. of Asian fish sauce, low sodium
- 1 head of lettuce, iceberg
- 1/2 cup of rice crackers, Asian

Instructions:

1. Place the green beans on a large piece of foil. Fold it in half. Crimp edges and seal the foil packet. Place on the grill beside flank steak. Cook for 10-12 minutes and turn once while cooking. Open the packet and cool the beans.

2. Cut the steak in 1/2" chunks and toss with cilantro, mint leaves, onion, tomatoes and green beans. Add fish sauce and soy vinaigrette.

3. Divide lettuce leaves on individual plates. Top with the steak mixture, then the rice crackers. Serve.

7 – Carne Asada Steak Tacos

This dish sounds extravagant but it's actually easy, and the flavor never lets you down. You may choose filet mignon, New York strip or top sirloin steaks to make this recipe great.

Makes 6 Servings

Cooking + Prep Time: 1 hour 20 minutes

Ingredients:

- 1 1/2 lbs. of bite-size-cubed beef top sirloin, boneless
- 1/2 tsp. of salt, kosher
- 1 tsp. of pepper, black, ground

- Red pepper, crushed, as desired
- 1 lime, fresh
- 1 x 28-oz. can of tomatillos
- 2 de-seeded jalapeno peppers, fresh
- 4 tbsp. of oil, canola
- 1 x 10 1/2 oz. can of broth, beef
- 12 x 6" tortillas, corn
- 1/2 chopped onion, large
- 2 chopped tomatoes
- 1 peeled, then pitted sliced avocado
- 1 bunch of chopped cilantro, fresh
- 1 lemon, fresh

Instructions:

1. Place the sliced meat in shallow bowl. Season as desired. Squeeze lime juice over steak. Make sure it is coated evenly. Cover. Place in fridge for 1/2 hour.

2. Combine jalapeno and tomatillo in food processor. Puree for about 15-20 seconds, till mixture thickens.

3. Heat 1 tbsp. of oil in large, heavy skillet on med-high. Pour in the tomatillo mixture carefully.

4. Stir frequently while cooking for five minutes. Add and stir beef broth into mixture. Reduce the heat. Simmer for 20-30 minutes, till mixture will coat a spoon. Transfer the mixture to serving dish.

5. Heat 1 tbsp. of oil in large sized skillet on high heat. Then add and stir 1/3 of steak. Sauté for a minute and transfer it to a serving dish. Repeat with the rest of the steak.

6. Heat the tortillas in microwave or oven, using instructions on the package.

7. Place two of the tortillas atop each other. Then add the amount of steak you prefer. Spoon on some of the tomatillo mixture. Top with cilantro, avocado, tomatoes and onions. Use lemon wedge to garnish and serve.

8 – Scallion Soy Flank Steak

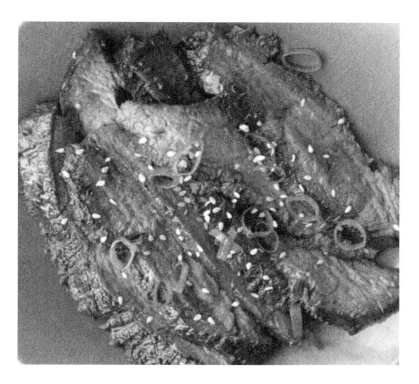

Flank steak is already kissed with great taste, and this marinade of delicious Asian ingredients will add new flavor to your grilled steak.

Makes 8 Servings

Cooking + Prep Time: 50 minutes + 2-8 hours marinating time

Ingredients:

- 1 cup of soy sauce, low sodium
- 3 garlic cloves
- 2 tbsp. of grated and peeled ginger, fresh
- 2 tbsp. of vinegar, rice
- 1 tbsp. of oil, Asian sesame
- 1 tbsp. of sugar, granulated
- 1/2 tsp. of cayenne pepper, ground
- 1 bunch of onions, green
- 2 1/2 pounds of flank steak, beef

Instructions:

1. Whisk the oil, vinegar, soy sauce, cayenne pepper, sugar, ginger and garlic in a medium sized bowl till sugar has dissolved. Reserve 2 tbsp. of the marinade. Cover it and set it aside. Transfer the rest of the marinade to a large, zipper lock plastic bag.

2. Slice green onions thinly and reserve 1/4 cup of them for garnishing. Add the rest of the green onions and the steak to the marinating bag. Seal the bag shut and press out any excess air from bag. Place marinating bag on a plate. Place

in fridge for two hours or the overnight. Turn a few times during the marinating period.

3. Prepare your grill for direct covered grilling over medium heat. Remove the steak from its marinade. Scrape off any excess solids and then place steak on the hot grill grate. Discard the leftover bagged marinade.

4. Cover the grill. Cook the steak for 12-14 minutes (med-rare) or till it is done to your desired level. Turn once while cooking. Allow steak to stand for 10 minutes. This allows the juices to set and **Makes** it easier to slice.

5. Combine 2 tbsp. of hot, filtered water with the reserved marinade and drizzle over the steak. Sprinkle on reserved green onions and serve.

9 – Braised Round Steak

This recipe features round beef steaks simmered in a sauce that includes red wine, till it is so tender you can cut it with just a fork.

Makes 6 Servings

Cooking + Prep Time: 1 1/2 hours

Ingredients:

- 2 tbsp. of oil, vegetable
- 2 sliced onions, large
- 12 x 4-oz. round steaks, beef eye

- 1/4 tsp. of thyme, dried
- 1 tsp. of salt, seasoned
- 1/4 cup of flour, all-purpose, to coat
- 1 cup of consommé, beef
- 1 cup of wine, Burgundy
- 1 tsp. of chopped parsley, fresh

Instructions:

1. Heat oil in large, heavy skillet on med-high. Add the onions. Stir while cooking till they are tender and lightly browned. Remove onions from skillet with slotted spoon. Put them in small bowl and set the bowl aside.

2. Season steaks as desired. Lightly dust with the flour. Fry steaks in same skillet, on med-high till both sides are browned.

3. Pour beef consommé and red wine in skillet with steak. Return cooked onions to skillet, as well. Cook on med-high till wine aroma has dissipated.

4. Reduce the heat level to low. Cover the skillet and simmer for about an hour. Pour sauce over steaks, sprinkle with parsley and serve.

10 – Steak Mushroom Sauce

Ah, the union of pan-fried filet mignon steak and a port, mushroom and shallot sauce. Tawny or ruby port brings the flavors out wonderfully.

Makes 4 Servings

Cooking + Prep Time: 35 minutes

Ingredients:

- 4 filet mignon steaks, well-trimmed
- 1/2 tsp. of salt, kosher
- 1/4 tsp. of pepper, black, ground

- 1 tsp. of oil, olive
- 1 shallot, large
- 1 pkg. of sliced mushrooms, white
- 1 pkg. of assorted sliced mushrooms, wild
- 1/4 cup of wine, port

Instructions:

1. Sprinkle the steaks over both sides using 1/4 tsp. of kosher salt and 1/8 tsp. of ground pepper. Heat a non-stick skillet on med-high till quite hot.

2. Add the steaks. Cook for eight-10 minutes, turning once, if you like your steaks done medium-rare. Leave on longer if you like them done med-well or well-done. Transfer the steaks to a platter and keep them warm.

3. Add oil and the shallot to skillet drippings. Stir often while cooking for a minute. Add the mushrooms season as desired. Cook and stir frequently till the liquid has evaporated and the mushroom mixture appears golden.

4. Add 1/4 cup of filtered water and the port wine. Cook for 1/2 minute while constantly stirring. Spoon the mushroom sauce on steaks. Serve.

11 – Flank Steak Bulgogi

Steak Bulgogi is a Korean based treat that can be simply rolled in leaf lettuce, with hot pepper paste and rice. Adding red pepper powder will spice it up even more.

Makes 4 Servings

Cooking + Prep Time: 20 minutes + 1-8 hours refrigeration time

Ingredients:

- 1 lb. of thinly sliced flank steak
- 5 tbsp. of soy sauce, low sodium
- 2 1/2 tbsp. of sugar, granulated
- 1/4 cup of green onions, chopped
- 2 tbsp. each of minced garlic, sesame seeds and sesame oil
- 1/2 tsp. of black pepper, ground

Instructions:

1. Place steak in shallow dish. Combine the soy sauce, pepper, sesame oil, sesame seeds, garlic, green onions and sugar in small sized bowl and pour the mixture over the steak.

2. Cover. Refrigerate for one hour minimum, or, for best results, overnight.

3. Preheat your grill for high level of heat. Oil grate lightly.

4. Grill steak quickly on grill till cooked through and charred slightly. Serve.

12 – Tuscan Style Steak with Beans

This Tuscan style top loin steak is seasoned with vinegar, rosemary and onion. It is left so tender that it almost literally melts in your mouth.

Makes 4 Servings

Cooking + Prep Time: 25 minutes

Ingredients:

- 1 tsp. of oil, olive
- 2 top loin beef steaks, boneless
- 1/2 tsp. of salt, kosher
- 1/2 tsp. of pepper, ground coarsely

- 1 onion, medium
- 1 cup of vinegar, balsamic
- 2 tsp. of rosemary, fresh + fresh leaves
- 1 pint of tomatoes, cherry or grape
- 1 can of kidney beans, white

Instructions:

1. Heat oil on med-high in heavy skillet till quite hot – not yet smoking, though. Season steaks as desired. Add them to the skillet. Cook and turn once for eight-10 minutes for med-rare, or until done to your desired level. Keep the steaks warm.

2. Reduce the heat down to med. Add the onion to skillet drippings. Cook and stir till they are tender and brown. Add 2 tbsp. of water, vinegar and rosemary. Stir till you have loosened any brown bits from skillet bottom.

3. Add and stir beans and tomatoes. Cook and occasionally stir for two minutes till they are heated through.

4. Slice steaks thinly. Use rosemary leaves to garnish. Serve with bean and tomato mixture.

13 – London Broil

When you want to craft a fancy meal that is also easy on the budget, a London Broil has been a family go-to for years. I can purchase an affordable cut of steak and enhance it through the London Broil cooking technique.

Makes 8 Servings

Cooking + Prep Time: 45 minutes + 5-8 hours marinating time

Ingredients:

- 1 minced garlic clove
- 1 tsp. of salt, kosher
- 3 tbsp. of soy sauce, low sodium
- 1 tbsp. of ketchup
- 1 tbsp. of oil, vegetable
- 1/2 tsp. of pepper, black, ground
- 1/2 tsp. of oregano, dried
- 4 lbs. of flank steak

Instructions:

1. Mix oil, ground pepper, oregano, ketchup, soy sauce, kosher salt and garlic together in small sized bowl.

2. Score meat on both sides with a diamond cut at 1/8" depth. Rub the garlic mixture in on both sides of steak. Wrap it tightly in foil. Refrigerate for five to six hours or leave it overnight. Flip the meat over every few hours or so.

3. Preheat grill for high level of heat. Oil the grate lightly.

4. Place steak on grill and cook for three to seven minutes on each side, or till it is done to your liking. Serve.

14 – Filet Mignon Roquefort

Filet mignon is such a lean and tender cut and cooking it in olive oil adds to the delectability. The luxurious Roquefort cheese on top is a flavor enhancer that creates an even tastier meal.

Makes 4 Servings

Cooking + Prep Time: 20 minutes

Ingredients:

- 2 tsp. of oil, olive
- 4 x 1" thick steaks, beef tenderloin

- 1/2 tsp. of salt, kosher
- 1/4 tsp. of pepper, ground coarsely
- 1 oz. of cheese, Roquefort

Instructions:

1. Heat oil over high heat in 12" skillet till it is hot.

2. Set steaks on wax paper sheet. Season both sides with 1/2 tsp. of kosher salt and 1/4 tsp. of ground pepper.

3. Add the steaks to the skillet. Cook 10 minutes, turning one time, if you prefer your steaks medium-rare, or until they are done to your liking.

4. Transfer the steaks to four individual plates and top them with Roquefort. Serve.

15 – Chicken Fried Beef Steak

I've been using this recipe for a few years now. It's the most flavorful chicken fried steak recipe I have ever tried. Even southern-raised people give it rave reviews.

Makes 4 Servings

Cooking + Prep Time: 45 minutes

Ingredients:

- 4 x 1/2-lb. cube steaks, beef
- 2 cups of flour, all-purpose
- 2 tsp. of baking powder

- 1 tsp. of baking soda
- 1 tsp. of pepper, ground, black
- 1 1/2 cups of buttermilk
- 3/4 tsp. of salt, kosher
- 1 egg, large
- 1 tbsp. of sauce, hot pepper
- 2 minced garlic cloves
- To dry fry: 3 cups of shortening, vegetable
- 1/4 cup of flour, all-purpose
- 4 cups of milk, 2%
- Salt, kosher, as desired
- Pepper, black, ground, as desired

Instructions:

1. Pound steaks to a thickness of roughly 1/4". Place two cups flour in shallow bowl.

2. Stir baking soda, baking powder, kosher salt and ground pepper in separate shallow bowl. Add and stir buttermilk, garlic, egg and hot sauce.

3. Dredge steaks in flour first, then batter, then back to flour. Pat flour onto surface of steaks so they're coated completely with flour.

4. Heat shortening in deep, heavy skillet up to 325F. Fry steaks till evenly a golden brown in color. This takes about three to five minutes on each side.

5. Drain the steaks on paper towels. Drain fat from skillet and reserve 1/4 cup of liquid and as many solids as you can.

6. Return skillet to med-low with reserved oil. Whisk remaining flour into oil. Scrape bottom of pan to release any solids up into gravy. Add and stir milk and raise heat up to med. Bring gravy to simmer, then cook till it has thickened, or six to seven minutes.

7. Season gravy and steaks as desired. Spoon gravy over steaks and serve.

16 – Taco Salad with Steak

This is a healthy salad that unites taco basics and transforms them into a family-friendly, healthy dish. You can also sub pork tenderloin or grilled chicken breasts for the beef steak.

Makes 4 Servings

Cooking + Prep Time: 1/2 hour

Ingredients:

- 4 tortillas, corn
- 8 green onions
- 2 cups of cabbage
- 1 flank steak, grilled
- 1 jicama (Mexican turnip), small
- 1 tomato, ripe
- 1 cup of lime cilantro dressing

Instructions:

1. Place the green onions beside flank steak on your grill. Cook for eight to 10 minutes, till the beans are mostly charred. Cool them and trim the ends. Cut in 1" pieces.

2. Next, place the onions in large sized bowl with chopped tomato, sliced jicama and the lime and cilantro dressing. Toss and coat evenly.

3. Place a corn tortilla between two sheets of paper towels. Microwave on the high setting for one minute or so, till crisp and golden. Repeat with the other tortillas.

4. Place one tortilla on each individual plate. Top with a half a cup of shredded cabbage. Divide the jicama mixture and steak (slice thinly) on all the tortillas. Serve.

17 – Cilantro-Lime Marinated Steak

This marinated steak works wonderfully in fajitas, as a main dish or appetizer. It **Makes** good sandwiches, too. Reserve some marinade for a delectable sauce.

Makes 9 Servings

Cooking + Prep Time: 25 minutes + 8 hours of marinating time

Ingredients:

- 6 garlic cloves
- 1/2 chopped onion, red
- 2 fresh limes, juice only
- 1 jalapeno pepper, medium
- 2 tbsp. of thyme leaves, fresh
- 1 cup of cilantro leaves, packed loosely
- 3/4 cup of oil, corn
- 2 tbsp. of honey, pure
- 3 lbs. of flank steak, beef
- Salt, kosher, as desired

Instructions:

1. Puree honey, corn oil, cilantro, thyme, jalapeno, lime juice, onion and garlic into your food processor. Blend till incorporated well.

2. Marinate steak in 1/2 cup of puree in zipper lock plastic bag in refrigerator overnight. Reserve remainder of puree to use at a later date for sauce.

3. Preheat your grill for med-high.

4. As grill warms, remove meat from fridge. Allow to set out at room temp. for 1/2 hour or longer. Discard excess marinade.

5. Season steak liberally with salt. Cook till done as you desire.

6. For serving, slice steak against grain in 1/4-1/8" slices. Drizzle the rest of the marinade over meat. Serve.

18 – Tri-Tip Steak Horseradish Cream

The wonderfully seasoned tri-tip steak stands front and center in this delicious meal. Add a side dish of roasted potatoes and serve for special occasions or everyday dinners.

Makes 6 Servings

Cooking + Prep Time: 50 minutes

Ingredients:

- 4 garlic cloves
- 2 fresh rosemary sprigs
- 1 tsp. + 1 tbsp. of oil, olive
- Salt, kosher
- Pepper, ground
- 1 1/2 pounds of potatoes
- 1 roast, sirloin tip (tri-tip), whole
- 1/4 cup of heavy cream
- 2 tbsp. of horseradish, prepared
- 1/2 tsp. of mustard, Dijon
- 1/2 tsp. of vinegar, white wine

Instructions:

1. Preheat the oven to 475F. Smash three garlic cloves gently and discard the peel. Crush the last clove into small sized bowl with a garlic press.

2. Cut one of the rosemary sprigs into 1" pieces and set them aside. Remove the leaves from the second sprig and discard the stem. Chop the leaves finely. Add to the crushed garlic bowl, with 1 tsp. of oil 1/4 tsp. each of kosher salt and ground pepper. Set the bowl aside.

3. Combine the potatoes, smashed garlic, 1 tbsp. of oil, 1/4 tsp. of kosher salt and 1/4 tsp. of ground pepper in 12"x18" pan till mixed well. Spread it evenly, creating a space in the middle of the pan for the steak.

4. Place steak in middle of pan with the fat side facing down. Rub it with your reserved rosemary and garlic mixture.

5. Roast for 20 minutes, till the steak has browned. Lower oven heat to 350F. Roast for eight to 10 minutes, till internal temperature is 130F. Transfer the steak to a cutting board and cover it loosely. Allow it to stand for about 10 minutes, then transfer the potatoes to a platter.

6. Whisk the vinegar, cream, mustard, horseradish, 1/8 tsp. of kosher salt and 1/8 tsp. of ground pepper till blended well. Thinly slice meat. Serve it with horseradish cream and potatoes.

19 – Slow Cooker Style Pepper Steak

This recipe is a family favorite, with its flavorful and tender treatment of steak. You can make it the day before in a slow cooker, if you like. It tastes great over rice or egg noodles.

Makes 6 Servings

Cooking + Prep Time: 35 minutes + 3-4 hours slow cooker time

Ingredients:

- 2 lbs. of 2" strip-cut beef sirloin steak
- Garlic powder, as desired
- 3 tbsp. of oil, vegetable
- 1 beef bouillon cube
- 1/4 cup of hot, filtered water
- 1 tbsp. of corn starch
- 1/2 cup of onion, chopped
- 2 chopped bell peppers, green, large
- 1 14 1/2 oz. can of tomatoes, stewed, with their liquid
- 3 tbsp. of soy sauce, low sodium
- 1 tsp. of sugar, granulated
- 1 tsp. of salt, kosher

Instructions:

1. Sprinkle the sirloin strips with the garlic powder, as desired. In large sized skillet on med., heat oil. Brown steak strips and transfer them to your slow cooker.

2. Mix hot water and bouillon cube till the cube dissolves. Add corn starch and mix till it dissolves, as well. Add to slow cooker. Then add soy sauce, stewed tomatoes, green peppers, onion, salt and sugar.

3. Cover. Cook on the high setting for three to four hours. Remove and serve hot.

20 – Sesame Steak

This flavorful, simple steak stir-fry takes just a little over a half-hour to prepare. It's a delicious but quick way to put dinner on the table for the family or guests.

Makes 4 Servings

Cooking + Prep Time: 35 minutes

Ingredients:

- 1 pound of steak, rib-eye
- 1 cup of rice, jasmine or short-grain

- 2 scallions
- 4 garlic cloves
- 4 tsp. of oil, Asian sesame
- 1/4 tsp. of salt, kosher
- 2 tsp. of sugar, granulated
- 2 tbsp. of soy sauce, low sodium
- 1 pound of broccoli florets
- Salt, kosher
- Pepper, ground

Instructions:

1. Place the steak in your freezer. Prepare the rice using instructions on package.

2. Combine 1 tbsp. of sliced scallions, 2 tsp. of oil, 1/4 tsp. of salt and 1 tsp. of garlic in large sized bowl and set the bowl aside.

3. Cut the chilled steak across the grain in thin slices. In a shallow type bowl, toss it with scallion chunks, 1 tbsp. of soy sauce, sugar and the rest of the garlic.

4. Heat 1" of filtered water to a boil in 12" skillet over high heat. Add the broccoli florets. Cook for three minutes, till

barely tender. Drain the florets well. Place in bowl with garlic and onion mixture. Toss and combine.

5. Heat the last of the oil in the same 12" skillet over high, till hot. Add the steak in one layer. Cook for a minute. Add and stir remaining scallions and season as desired. Cook for another minute. Add and stir the rest of the soy sauce and serve with broccoli and rice.

21 – Mojo Grilled Steak

The marinade in this recipe is inspired by those of Cuba, and you can use it as a marinade for all kinds of grilled food. It enhances steak the best though, I think.

Makes 4 Servings

Cooking + Prep Time: 1 hour 20 minutes + 2-3 hours refrigeration time

Ingredients:

- 2 lbs. of skirt steak, beef
- Juice from 1 navel orange, large
- 3 juiced limes, fresh
- 1/4 cup oil, olive + extra to drizzle
- 6 minced garlic cloves
- 1 tbsp. of salt, kosher
- 1 1/2 tsp. of cumin, ground
- 1 tsp. of pepper, black, ground
- 1/2 tsp. of oregano, dried
- 1/2 tsp. of pepper, cayenne
- 1/2 sliced onion
- 1/2 cup of cilantro, chopped
- To finish: 1 tsp. of salt, coarse
- To serve: lime wedges, fresh cut

Instructions:

1. Cut the steaks into three or four small sized pieces, so they are easier to work with.

2. Whisk the lime juice, orange juice, olive oil, cayenne pepper, oregano, ground pepper, cumin, kosher salt and garlic together in large sized bowl.

3. Place steak pieces, one after another, in marinade and coat well. Add the sliced onions. Toss them with steak.

4. Transfer marinade and mixture to zipper lock bag. Squeeze out the air and zip the bag shut. Place the bag on plate and refrigerate for two to three hours.

5. Transfer steak pieces to a cookie sheet lined with paper towels, so they can drain for a few minutes.

6. Cook the steak above hot coals. The first side should be grilled for three to four minutes. Flip the steaks and grill the other side till internal temperature is 125F or higher. You should see a glossy, shiny surface, which indicates that the juice of the meat is working its way up to its surface. That means the steaks are almost done.

7. Transfer steak to plate. Allow it to rest for several minutes.

8. Slice steak into 1/2" slices. Arrange them on serving platter. Spoon the juices over steak. Use oil to drizzle and sprinkle with cilantro and coarse salt. Place lime wedges beside the steak and serve.

22 – Chipotle Flatiron Steak Sandwiches

This recipe allows you to figuratively pump up any steak sandwich (I use flatiron steaks) with a mayo that is spiced with chipotle. We serve it with a ginger-enhanced cucumber salad.

Makes 4 Servings

Cooking + Prep Time: 35 minutes

Ingredients:

- 1/4 cup of mayonnaise, light
- 1/4 tsp. of chili powder, chipotle
- 1 pound of 1" thick flatiron steak
- Salt, kosher
- Pepper, black, ground
- 1 sweet onion, medium
- 1 tbsp. of water
- 1 cucumber, large
- 1 tbsp. of lemon juice, fresh
- 1/2 tsp. of grated and peeled ginger, fresh
- 2 ciabatta rolls

Instructions:

1. Combine mayo and chili powder in small sized bowl and set it aside.

2. Heat heavy skillet over med-high till quite hot. Season the steak as desired. Cook 12-15 minutes if you like medium doneness level. Cook longer if you like your meat well-done. Transfer the steak to a cutting board and let it sit.

3. Add water, onion 1/8 tsp. of salt to the same skillet. Reduce the heat down to med-low. Cook onion and stir for five to seven minutes, till it is tender.

4. In a medium sized bowl, toss ginger, lemon juice, cucumber and 1/8 tsp. of kosher salt till mixed well.

5. Slice the steak, across the grain. Spread the chili mayo on the rolls. Top with the steak and onions. Serve alongside cucumber salad.

23 – Skillet Pepper Steak

This recipe is a no-brainer for me because it uses ingredients I usually have on-hand already. In addition, it's really hard to screw this dinner up. You can adjust the ingredients to suit the tastes of your family or guests.

Makes 4 Servings

Cooking + Prep Time: 55 minutes

Ingredients:

- 2 tbsp. of oil, olive
- 1 chopped onion, medium
- 2 strip-sliced large peppers, bell
- 2 minced garlic cloves
- 1/3 cup of soy sauce, low sodium
- 1/3 cup of honey, pure
- 1/3 cup of vinegar, red wine
- 1 1/2 lbs. of thinly sliced flank steak

Instructions:

1. Heat oil in skillet on med. heat. Cook the garlic, onion and bell peppers in the oil and stir frequently till they are tender-crisp. Set them aside.

2. Heat large sized skillet on med-high. Add soy sauce, red wine vinegar and honey. Add steak. Cook the steak and stir frequently till it is done. This will take 10-15 minutes. Add and stir cooked veggies. Cook for 12-15 additional minutes. Serve hot.

24 – Chili Steak Hawaiian Rice

This meal takes less than a half-hour to prepare, so it's high on flavor and low on work. You can use leftover cooked rice to serve under the chili steak.

Makes 4 Servings

Cooking + Prep Time: 25 minutes

Ingredients:

- 1 1/2 pound of steak, skirt
- 2 tsp. of chili powder
- 1 1/2 tsp. of lime peel, grated

- 1 lime, fresh, whole
- 1/2 tsp. of salt, kosher
- 2 cups of chopped pineapple, fresh
- 1 cup of chopped, packed cilantro leaves, fresh
- 3 cups of white rice, cooked

Instructions:

1. Heat your grill on med-high.

2. Rub steak with salt, chili powder and lime peel. Grill steak for three to four minutes on each side, till it is done to your liking.

3. Transfer steak to cutting board. Allow to set for five minutes. Toss the pineapple with white rice and cilantro leaves.

4. Slice steak thinly. Garnish with the lime wedges. Serve with cooked rice.

25 – Ginger Soy Rib-Eye Steaks

This marinade is a wonder on good-quality steaks, and it also tenderizes cheaper cuts of meat. You can even use it for stir-fry dishes.

Makes 4 Servings

Cooking + Prep Time: 1 1/2 hours

Ingredients:

- 1/2 cup soy sauce, low sodium
- 1/4 cup of maple syrup, pure
- 6 minced garlic cloves

- 1 tbsp. of grated ginger, fresh
- 1 tsp. of powdered mustard
- 1/2 tsp. oil, sesame
- 1/4 tsp. pepper sauce, hot
- 1/2 cup of beer, your preferred brand
- 4 x 10-oz. rib-eye steaks, beef

Instructions:

1. Combine the sesame oil, hot sauce, mustard powder, ginger, garlic, syrup and soy sauce in medium bowl. Mix and blend well.

2. Add the beer. Stir a bit to combine ingredients.

3. Prepare the steaks by scoring fatty exterior areas on the steak using a knife.

4. Place steaks in baking dish. Pour the marinade over it. Use a fork to punch holes in the steaks, to help marinade penetrate into steaks. Turn the steaks over. Punch holes on the other side, as well.

5. Cover the steaks and marinade with foil or cling wrap. Allow it to marinate in your refrigerator for an hour or more. Leaving it overnight is fine.

6. Prepare the grill for high heat. Place steaks on grill. Sear the first side for 15 seconds. Then turn steaks over and cook for five more minutes. Turn steaks yet again and cook for five more minutes if you prefer medium-rare. Test for how done the steak is by cutting into its middle portion. Serve.

26 – Steak with Fingerling Fries

This is a wonderful recipe, since it takes something you usually eat in a restaurant and allows you to make it at home. The simple bistro classic is very delicious and tastes as good as you might eat on a night on the town.

Makes 4 Servings

Cooking + Prep Time: 35 minutes

Ingredients:

- 1 pound of potatoes, fingerling
- 2 x 1"-thick steaks, strip
- 2 tbsp. of unsalted butter, softened

- 1 tbsp. of pesto, prepared
- Oil, kosher salt and ground pepper

Instructions:

1. Heat the oven to 450F. Scrub the potatoes with plain water. Quarter them lengthways. They should be the same general shape as steak fries.

2. On rimmed, large sized cookie sheet, toss the potatoes with 1 tbsp. of oil 1/4 tsp. of kosher salt. Transfer to oven. Roast till fries are a golden-brown color. This takes 18-20 minutes, typically.

3. Season the steaks with 1/2 tsp. each kosher salt ground pepper. Heat 12" skillet on med-high for one minute. Add 1 tbsp. of oil and add steaks to skillet. Cook till the steak is done to your liking. Three minutes per side will cook them to med-rare. Transfer cooked steak to cutting board. Allow to rest for five minutes before you slice it.

4. Combine 2 tbsp. of butter with 1 tbsp. of pesto in small sized bowl. Serve steaks with French fries pesto butter.

27 – Marinated Korean Style Flank Steak

A marinade that works well on any steak, this one is especially great for flank steak. It came from Korea and it's a meal that is easier to prepare than you would think.

Makes 6 Servings

Cooking + Prep Time: 35 minutes + 8 hours marinating time

Ingredients:

- 4 garlic cloves
- 1 tsp. of minced ginger, fresh
- 1 chopped onion, medium
- 2 1/2 cups of soy sauce, low sodium
- 1/4 cup of sesame oil, toasted
- 3 tbsp. of Worcestershire sauce, reduced sodium
- 2 tbsp. of meat tenderizer, unseasoned
- 1 cup of sugar, granulated
- 2 lbs. of flank steak, beef, with excess fat trimmed

Instructions:

1. Place the onion, garlic and ginger in blender bowl. Add the sugar, tenderizer, Worcestershire sauce, sesame oil and soy sauce. Puree till you have a smooth texture.

2. Pour marinade in zipper lock plastic bag. Score steak. Place in marinade. Marinate in fridge overnight.

3. Preheat grill for med-high.

4. Grill the steak to the level of doneness you desire, which takes roughly six or seven minutes each side for medium doneness. Serve.

28 – Beet Onion Steak Salad

This recipe uses a sous vide machine, which is being used by more and more people who cook great steak dishes at home. It will help you create the juiciest steak salad you have ever tasted.

Makes 4 Servings

Cooking + Prep Time: 40 minutes

Ingredients:

- 1 x 2-inch thick top loin beef steak, boneless
- 1 tbsp. of oil, vegetable
- 1/2 bunch of halved green onions

- 3/4 tsp. of salt, sea, flaky
- 1 x 5-ounce container of greens, mixed
- 1/2 small head of radicchio, with separated and torn leaves
- 4 quartered beets, cooked
- 1/4 cup of vinegar, red wine
- 1 tbsp. of oil, olive
- 2 ounces of crumbled blue cheese

Instructions:

1. Set up your sous vide device by instructions on package in eight-quart sauce pot. Add filtered water. Set the temperature on device to 130F.

2. Place the steak in zipper lock bag. Tightly seal. Release excess air. Place the bag in the hot water and cook for two hours.

3. Remove the bag from hot water. Remove the steak from the bag and pat it dry.

4. In a 10-inch skillet, heat the oil over med-high till quite hot. Add the green onions. Cook for two minutes, and turn, till lightly charred.

5. Add the steak to the skillet. Cook for two minutes while frequently turning. Transfer steak to a cutting board. Sprinkle with 1/2 tsp. of sea salt. Slice thickly.

6. Toss the olive oil, vinegar, beets, radicchio, greens and 1/4 tsp. each sea salt and ground pepper together in a large sized bowl. Transfer mixture to a platter. Top with the onions, steak and blue cheese. Serve.

29 – Garlic Steak

The "secret" to this recipe is NO secret – garlic and more garlic, and a good cut of steak. Garlic fans will smile and savor the results of your efforts.

Makes 2 Servings

Cooking + Prep Time: 50 minutes + 8 hours marinating time

Ingredients:

- 8 minced garlic cloves
- 1 tbsp. of oil, olive

- A pinch each of salt, kosher, and pepper, ground + more as desired
- 2 x 12-oz. New York strip steaks
- 12 peeled garlic cloves
- To fry: 1 cup of oil, olive
- 1 1/2 tbsp. of vinegar, balsamic

Instructions:

1. Whisk the olive oil, minced garlic, kosher salt ground pepper in medium bowl. Pour into zipper lock bag.

2. Add the steaks and coat them with marinade. Squeeze excess air out. Seal bag. Marinate in fridge overnight.

3. Combine the 12 peeled cloves of garlic and a cup of oil in small sized sauce pan on low heat. Stir occasionally while cooking, till the garlic is tender and golden. Set it aside.

4. Preheat your grill for high level heat. Oil grate lightly. Remove the steaks from their bag. Wipe excess marinade off with paper towels. Season the steaks generously as desired.

5. Cook steaks on grill, till they begin firming up and are juicy and red-pink in center. Interior temperature should be 130F or higher.

6. Remove the steaks to plate. Allow to rest for five minutes. Drizzle the steaks with balsamic steaks. Spoon in several oil-roasted garlic cloves on the top. Serve.

30 – Smoky, Sweet Tri-Tip

This recipe uses the tri-tip, which is the triangular meat at the base of the sirloin. It's a wonderful cut of meat and the taste is even better when you use a brown sugar and paprika rub.

Makes 8 Servings

Cooking + Prep Time: 55 minutes

Ingredients:

- 1 tbsp. each of oil, olive; brown sugar; ground cumin; smoked paprika

- 1 tsp. each garlic and onion powders
- 1 tri-tip beef roast, boneless

Instructions:

1. Heat the grill on the medium setting.

2. Combine the oil, garlic and onion powder, paprika, cumin, sugar, 2 tsp. of kosher salt 1/2 tsp. of ground pepper. Rub this over all areas of the steak.

3. Grill the steak for 1/2 hour or till inside temperature is 125F. Turn three times while grilling. Transfer steak to a cutting board and allow it to rest for 10 minutes or more. Slice thinly against the grain and serve.

Conclusion

This steak cookbook has shown you…

How to use different ingredients to affect unique tastes in steak-centered dishes both well-known and rare.

How can you include steak in your home recipes?

You can…

- Make steak and eggs for a wonderful, special breakfast for you and your family. It is just as tasty as you have heard.
- Learn to cook with steak rubs, which are widely used in cooking and grilling steaks. You can make all types of flavored rubs.
- Enjoy making the delectable seafood and steak dishes, including salmon, mackerel and shrimp. Fish goes well with steak, and there are SO many ways to make it great.
- Make dishes using all kinds of vegetables, which are often used in steak preparation.

- Make various types of marinades to elevate your steaks to a higher level and tempt your family's appetite.

Have fun experimenting! Enjoy the results!

Printed in Great Britain
by Amazon